REDESIGN

REDESIGN

Becoming a Happy, Healthy,
and Successful Entrepreneur

SEBASTIAAN HOOFT

REDESIGN
*Becoming a Happy, Healthy,
and Successful Entrepreneur*

ISBN   978-1-54450-136-9   *Paperback*
       978-1-61961-596-0   *Ebook*

INTERIOR DESIGN BY
Kevin Barrett Kane

LIONCREST
PUBLISHING

TABLE OF CONTENTS

MY NEAR-DEATH EXPERIENCE

THE LIGHTS WERE SO BRIGHT, blinding even. I opened my eyes further. Where was I? Then I smelled that familiar antiseptic odor. Oh, shit. I realized that I was lying in a bed in a hospital. Everyone reaches a moment when they realize that their life has been cut into two parts: before and after. This was my moment. Waking up in that hospital, I knew that my life had changed forever.

Up until then, by all appearances, I had been living the life of a rock star entrepreneur in the Netherlands. I was on the financial magazine *Quote*'s "Young Rich List," which charts the five hundred wealthiest, self-made entrepreneurs under forty years old in my country. I had other successful businesses. I was constantly being interviewed by the media. Just about everywhere I went, people recognized me.

It was 2009, I was in my midthirties, and at that point in time, I didn't realize that I was digging my own grave. I worked from six in the morning until midnight, seven days a week. I never took breaks. I was constantly on the phone, texting or talking, or on my computer. Everything I did was about growing my companies. I was rewarded for that because everything was great from a financial perspective. But the more my companies grew, the less of an individual I became. Meanwhile, I was out of shape and grossly overweight. Often, I would have two business meetings in one evening so I would just go to dinner twice. Everything I ate was comprised of fat, salt, and sugar.

When I did something besides work, I felt guilty. My girlfriend—well, actually now my ex-girlfriend—finally said to me, "Next time we get invited to one of my friends' birthday parties, maybe you should just stay home. All you talk about is work. It bores people." I didn't realize I had turned into this really annoying guy. (Although once I got on the *Quote* Junior 500 list, people did want me at their birthday parties just so they could tell their friends that I had been there. But nobody knew who I really was primarily because I didn't know who I really was either.)

So I ended up doing everything by myself. That's not how we're wired as human beings. We're social beings who need both one another and a sense of equilibrium. I started to plummet into an abyss—physically, mentally, and emotionally. By the time I ended up in the hospital, which, by the way, was a mental hospital, I had stopped eating. I had stopped drinking. I had stopped sleeping. You can't keep doing that for even a short time. Eventually, you will fall—hard. And that's what happened. It was total burnout. And my purpose in writing this book is to help you avoid the same state.

So this isn't a sad story about my nervous breakdown. It's also not an inspirational memoir about a Dutch phoenix rising from the ashes. When I say I want to help you avoid the same fate, I'm assuming you picked up this book because you're an entrepreneur, or a would-be entrepreneur, who wants it all: financial and creative success plus a fulfilling personal life. And so far, you haven't been able to find a way to do that. Most people think you can have one or the other. I want you to have both, and I'm going to show you how.

Meanwhile, there's not a whole lot to do when you're in the hospital except think. After a couple of months, I started thinking one thought: *Why are we here on earth?*

I asked myself this question morning, noon, and night. After a while, I had a breakthrough.

I started to think about the way lions live their lives. I know this may sound weird because I'm a guy, but in this case, I was thinking about the lioness because she's the hunter of the pride.

She hunts for food when she and the other lions are hungry. When they're not hungry, she just has a nice, relaxed time in the sun. I realized that if we could just spend our days as humans the way a lioness spends hers, we'd be happy. I came to the personal realization that we are here on the planet to have a comfortable life, a high-quality life. And that being in the hospital meant I was not living one. Being in the hospital meant my current life sucked.

So at that moment, I flipped the switch in my head. I told myself, *From today on, I'm going to live a happy life. I'm going to be that lion that wakes up and goes outside and just lies in the sun.*

I was out of the hospital in two weeks.

I can guarantee you that every day since then, I wake up and keep my promise to myself. Sure, sometimes I have to hunt for food, and sometimes another animal comes into my territory and threatens me, and I have to deal with that. I still make a lot of mistakes. But I changed for good.

I meet people all the time who say things like, "I'm miserable at work, so I'm going to find another job with people who are friendlier, people who treat me with respect." Or, "My relationship isn't working anymore, so I'm going to have an affair." Or, "When my kids leave the house, that's when I'll come alive, that's when my real life will start."

It's always about trying to get something outside yourself. It's always a distraction from what's really important. My nine months of suffering in the hospital ended with a one-minute thought. What I realized in the hospital, and what has shaped my life ever since, is this: it is not human nature to be unhappy. Aristotle knew this. He was convinced that a genuinely happy life required the fulfillment of a broad range of conditions, including physical as well as mental well-being. He introduced the idea of a science of happiness in the classical sense, in terms of a new field of knowledge and a new way of being.

AN ENTIRELY NEW CHAPTER

I left the hospital on a beautiful spring day. For the rest of the world, nothing had happened. But my entire universe had shifted. I knew my social environment would try and draw me back into being the person I used to be, and I would need to do everything possible to push back. Step by step, I started redesigning my life.

But if I'm going to be your tour guide on your journey to becoming a happy, healthy, and successful entrepreneur, you need to know a little bit more about how I got to where I am.

So I'm going to briefly rewind.

I grew up in a little suburb outside Amsterdam called Uithoorn. It's your typical bedroom community. The place is quiet; nothing really happens—everyone's in Amsterdam working during the day. We've got two shopping malls and several parks full of new moms with their kids, as well as older people enjoying their retirements. Uithoorn is so small that we don't even have a tram or a trolley, just a single bus station.

Like most guys, my relationship with my dad was pivotal. When I was a kid, my dad would always say, "Sebastiaan, if you get the chance to be an entrepreneur, grab it because it's better to work for yourself than anyone else."

My dad had a job at IBM as a business analyst. He felt like he couldn't leave because the pay was great, and he needed the money to support his family. But before he worked at IBM, he was a pinball machine entrepreneur. He got into it first as a technician. He and a friend would buy these vintage wooden pinball machines from bars and cafés and refurbish them. At the time, these machines were really hot. My dad's clients were rock stars, pop stars, the rich, and the famous across many different spectrums. When we would drive through the city, my dad would point out all the amazing houses where his customers lived.

One day, he and his partner decided they should consider getting into the business of selling new machines. They called Bally, which back then was one of the world's biggest manufacturers of them. They made an appointment and went abroad to the main factory for a meeting.

The head guy at the factory asked my dad and his partner, "OK, how many do you want to buy?"

They mulled it over. "Well, maybe one or two a month," they replied.

"Well, that's fantastic," the man said. "We'll send you a confirmation, and it's done."

But when they received the confirmation, it turned out that they had contracted to purchase one or two *shipping containers* filled with pinball machines each month.

My dad backed out of the deal. There were probably fifty or more pinball machines in each container. He was just too scared he wouldn't be able to sell them.

"I should have bought the container," he'd always tell me when I was growing up. "Within a couple of months, we had to close our company because everyone else just got bigger and bigger, and we were just these little guys selling refurbished machines."

So again, what he'd always say to me as a kid was, "If you get a chance to be an entrepreneur, Sebastiaan, grab it." It almost became a mantra in my head.

Consequently, I started out as an entrepreneur when I was fourteen years old. I had a setup in my parents' house with two record players, a mixer, and a cassette deck. I made mixtapes with hard-core house music and sold them in the schoolyard. They sold like crazy. I had basically founded my own record label.

When I was eighteen, I started a venture that transcribed documents for companies and put them into WordPerfect format. The venture after that was selling computer gear out of a booth at a technology fair.

But a few years later, I found myself too isolated as an

entrepreneur. I didn't have a mentor to help me grow, and books like this one were rare at that time. So I decided to go work for someone else for a while. Like Steve Jobs and so many other entrepreneurs, I had quit college because I just wanted to learn what I wanted to learn. I got a job as an executive at Gartner, a big technology and research firm. I was giving C-level advice to technology companies on their strategy. I was making a lot of money at the time—about $120,000 a year—and I was only twenty-four years old.

On my first day at Gartner, I walked into the lobby, grabbed all these old magazines lying on the coffee table, threw them in the trash, and put down my own fresh copy of the Dutch *Financial Times* as a replacement. I thought, *Wow, this is cool. My first day, and I've already improved the office.* At lunch, I told the manager who hired me about it. An hour later, she called me into her office.

"Listen, Sebastiaan," she said, "we didn't hire you as our cleaning service, and we didn't hire you to deliver our newspaper. We hired you to bring in revenue, so stop throwing away our old magazines. Put them back."

Digging those old magazines out of the trash was demoralizing. On my first day, this prestigious firm that employs the smartest researchers you can find in my entire country broke me. It took me a year to learn that working for a company that breaks its employees on the first day is not an environment in which you will be happy. About a year later, one of my buddies at work died of a heart attack. He was forty years old. The next day, I quit my job. I said, "I am not going to have a heart attack working for other people. If I'm going to have a heart attack, it's because I'm working for me and not for someone else." Most of us become entrepreneurs not because we want to, but because something inside of us knows there's just no other option.

A FAST RISE

I was twenty-five, and I soon cofounded an Internet retailer that sold computer gear. It quickly became one of the biggest Dutch companies of its kind. We started the company in 2002, and by 2008, I was one of the richest people in the Netherlands.

I should have been on top of the world, but I wasn't. I never took one second to look at what we were achieving. When we received an award or reached a sales target, it was just an endorsement for me to work harder. I wish I had celebrated my wins. Today, when I mentor people, I try and make them aware of what they've already accomplished and what they have right now. The only thing I looked at was how we could grow faster, and it was never enough even though the company was increasing revenues every year. Even when we received one of our biggest honors—being chosen by accounting firm Deloitte as one of Europe's five hundred fastest-growing companies—I felt nothing inside. It was just another piece of information.

I eventually ended up parting ways with the company as part of my life redesign. Overall, I founded and invested in twenty companies from 2002 to 2010.

The reason I'm telling you all this is because I want to bring it back around to the day I left the hospital. I had some basic questions when I walked out that door into my new life:

How did I end up being so successful—what had defined my success?

How did I nearly destroy myself, and how can I keep it from happening again?

Those are the questions people always want answers to when I give talks today. Young people always want to know, "How can I end up on *Quote*'s or *Forbes*'s or some other financial magazine's rich list because I want a Porsche, I want a house, and I want all the benefits of being wealthy?" Older people who are in what I call the "rush hour" of life—juggling kids and jobs—want to know, "How do I survive the burnout that I feel happening? How do I survive the company I started that isn't doing that well, the complaining spouse at home, the (beloved but) annoying kids who are preventing me from doing my job?"

The first group is looking for a vitamin to boost their career. The second group is looking for a painkiller to help deal with an illness. Even though those are two different things, I've learned that if you go through the Five Facets of Sustainable Entrepreneurship that I'm going to outline in this book, your business will grow, and you will find equilibrium and (hopefully) happiness at the same time.

What I've learned, though, is that you can't change your life, you can't follow the Five Facets, you can't find wealth and balance simultaneously if you do not do one thing first. And that's to first make the decision to change your life. What stops people is accepting responsibility for the consequences of making that decision.

But take it from someone who ended up almost destroying his life from burnout and overwork: The consequences of not making the decision can be far worse. I flipped the switch, and you can, too.

LOOK FOR THE LIFE PRESERVER

Whenever we go through a crisis, it's hard to envision how we will ever find our way back out. But life is mysterious. Life will always throw you a life preserver, and you can use it to paddle for the shore. When I left the hospital, even though I'd had this breakthrough, I spent the next two years kind of wandering around. I was pretty lost. Then a friend involved in a start-up accelerator program asked me to help out.

For three months, I mentored young people who were working their asses off to build their start-ups. I'd been on my own for years, and I honestly didn't realize how much I had to contribute. That's one of the problems that can come with being an entrepreneur: getting isolated. Thinking you have to do everything on your own. Losing touch with what's happening with the outside world.

When I joined up with the start-up accelerator as its entrepreneur in residence, I felt like the kid in the *Jungle Book* who grows up with animals, and then he meets humans and realizes he's a human! Being around all those entrepreneurs and having the opportunity to significantly impact them, I learned that all my knowledge was useful to other people. I didn't know it at the time, but I was transitioning into being a mentor and a teacher.

I was happy advising start-ups and transferring my knowledge to the next generation. But somehow, I felt obliged to start a new business, mainly because everyone kept asking me when I was going to do so. On a trip to San Francisco, I saw all these great microroasteries like Blue Bottle Coffee Company and similar hipster places. I decided to open one myself in the Netherlands. But its purpose wasn't just to serve fantastic coffee in a beautiful place. It was a halfway house of sorts for creative people in transition. Some people had lost their jobs or gotten fired; others had experienced health problems and weren't ready to work full time. They would apply to come work at our roastery filling bags with coffee, serving people, and doing other tasks to run the place. They weren't paid, but they also weren't at home by themselves going crazy as they frantically searched job sites. They were working in a cool environment with lots of music, friendly people, and no pressure. It became a magnet for anyone who needed a place to help them get back in the game. People who had been out of work for more than three years found jobs within three months of connecting with our roastery.

But through the process of creating the roastery, I realized that I had a calling bigger than running a business itself. I had been developing the Five Facets of Sustainable Entrepreneurship ever since I teamed up with the accelerator program. I started to recognize that refining and sharing the process with others was my next venture and perhaps my most important one. I found so many books existed out there on entrepreneurship and how to build businesses, but they didn't address quality of life, as if your life and your business resided in two separate universes. My goal is to give you a paradigm and a way of thinking that will bridge both.

In order to develop the model in this book, I researched entrepreneurship at Stanford University and elsewhere. I conducted extensive workshops with university students in the Netherlands. I traveled the world interviewing five hundred entrepreneurs. Finally, I used my hard-won lessons from being an A-list entrepreneur for more than two decades. I have found the Five Facets will work no matter where you live, from the United States and Asia to Europe and the Middle East.

The most common mistake I see people make when they want success is being focused on what they want next. They'll tell me,

"I'm an accountant, but I want to be a gardener." Or, "I'm a small entrepreneur, but I want to be a bigger one." Everyone thinks when they get *there*, wherever "there" is, they'll be happy. But it never happens. Whenever you move to a new place, as most of us have learned by now, your problems travel with you like the clothes in your duffel bag. Start with what makes you healthy and happy first, and fit your business goals into that framework. It sounds counterintuitive and maybe even a little radical, but if you can make those two goals your foundation, you'll be living the life you're designed to live, not someone else's.

PART ONE

LEARNING TO REBALANCE

CHAPTER ONE

MY JOURNEY

MY GIRLFRIEND AND I WALKED into the lobby of a shooting range, and the room fell silent. We were in the middle of the Texas Panhandle, in a room full of cops polishing their guns. They were huge, taciturn dudes. You probably already know that everything in Texas—from steaks to women's hair—is bigger than anywhere else in the United States. These guys were large and in charge. All eyes focused on us. I don't think any of them had ever seen any Dutch people before.

We had arrived in Texas a couple of weeks earlier and had been just driving across the state, stopping in little towns, listening to country music, and getting a feel for things. When I saw the sign off the highway that said, "Amarillo Police Department

Shooting Range," I knew we had to pull over and check it out. Now I felt like Lucky Luke, the cartoon cowboy who chased down bandits in the Old West. Whenever Lucky Luke would walk into a saloon, all the singing, shouting, and piano playing would abruptly stop. That wasn't good news.

"Hi, we're from the Netherlands, and we're here to see your shooting range," I said with as much confidence as I could muster.

More silence. Then the room started to buzz. The police officers started to smile. They were so excited that we were interested in their world and proceeded to give us a tour. They offered to let us try out the shooting range, and (after a mandatory psychological test and some training), my girlfriend and I did. We didn't miss too many targets (I'm not sure why, as neither of us carry firearms). When we came back in the building, they presented us with a certificate. I am now probably the only guy in Amsterdam who possesses an Amarillo Police Department shooting license.

The way I ended up in Texas in the first place was just as weird. We headed there not long after my breakdown for a change of scenery. The trip came about because one night I was watching *Criminal Minds*—that CBS show about FBI profilers. It was an episode where they were driving a big, black SUV through a forest in Quantico, Virginia. That's where the academy is located where they train special agents. The cinematography in the show was so amazing and the landscape so compelling that I just started thinking about what it would be like to take a trip there. I began Googling everything I could about Quantico. The bottom line was that I realized I needed a different environment in order to figure out my next steps.

I jumped on the KLM airlines website to find out about fares to Virginia. But in typical, impulsive, entrepreneurial fashion, my plans quickly changed. A tourism ad for Texas popped up. I thought, *Texas, yeah, desert, cowboys, I'm there!*

"You're going to Texas?" my girlfriend asked me.

"Uh-huh," I said. She gave me a funny look, as if measuring my sanity.

"I'm going with you," she replied.

We landed in Dallas in midsummer. I'd never felt so much heat in my life, and it felt great (it rains constantly in the Netherlands). We wanted to travel light, so we brought only carry-ons. The agents at customs and immigration were suspicious about that and hassled us for a while. When we got to the rental car place, a friendly young guy was behind the counter. We told him our entire story, from *Criminal Minds* to being detained, and he said, "OK, I've got a great deal for you. Just make sure you have a trip you never forget." He gave us the lowest price he could for an economy car, and when we walked out to the lot to pick it up... he had given us a big, black, shiny, *Criminal Minds*-style SUV. We were on our way.

Texas was another stage in my learning how to rebalance. I'd never had more than two days off in my life. It was amazing living a normal existence—eating properly, sleeping at least eight hours a night, connecting with real people, and enjoying myself—as opposed to the insane, caffeine-fueled existence I had called a life a few years earlier. Texas was a detox and the beginning of a new chapter of traveling the world, visiting fifteen countries on three continents to learn as much as I could about entrepreneurship.

It was in Texas that I learned about the impact a culture of generosity and community can have on you. One day, for example, we got a flat tire in the middle of nowhere. The state has miles and miles of nowhere.

On the side of the road stood a farmhouse and a huge, dirty-white barn with gray doors. I approached it, hoping to find someone to help us. But the entire place had the weirdest, scariest vibe. The door to the barn was open, but it was so dark you could barely see anything inside, just the shadows of old farm equipment. The silence was deafening. It seemed like all the humans had disappeared, and inside were zombies waiting to eat us.

We walked back to the car and mulled the situation for about ten minutes. Then, from a distance, we saw a truck winding its way toward us, kicking up a cloud of dust that almost obscured it. The truck finally reached us and stopped fifteen meters behind our SUV. It had a large metal contraption on the back and tinted glass so you couldn't see inside. Again, the whole thing felt like a horror movie. The truck just sat there for a few minutes. We thought, *Are we gonna be shot?*

The door opened. A gigantic guy hoisted himself out. He ambled to the back of the truck, grabbed a tool kit, and walked over to our car.

"Flat tire?" he grunted.

"Yeah," we said.

"Do you know how to change it?"

"No, sorry."

The guy did everything for us; we didn't even know where the spare tire was. The whole time he was fixing our flat I was thinking about how by the time I landed in the hospital, I had been working for fifteen years in the Netherlands, and yet not a single person showed up to help me in my darkest hour. Here now in the middle of nowhere in Texas, a complete stranger was going out of his way to give me a hand. It confronted me with the question, "What had I done so far in my life to help other people around me?"

As I watched that dude from Texas fix our car, I made the decision that I was going to give to other people without expecting something back. In the Dutch culture, most people, in my experience, think that's a weird thing to do. If I give something to you, you're supposed to automatically give something back. I'm sure the state of Texas has a lot of issues and they do plenty of stuff wrong, but it was there I learned what paying it forward means.

So, as I said, Texas was the beginning of a journey outside my country to research and refine the Five Facets of Sustainable Entrepreneurship. For the entire project, I found all the people I interviewed through referrals and serendipity. My criteria for locations were that I went primarily to sunny countries because it rains enough where I live.

Before my walkabout, I used to think of myself as a man of the world. I'd go on business trips to Japan, China, and the United States for a day or two and think I'd seen those places. But going to Texas, I learned how to get underneath the skin of a place. In order to understand a country, you have to connect with its people.

That's what happened to me on a trip to San Francisco, where I met the guy who became one of my best friends. On my first night there, the apartment where I was staying had bedbugs. I got in touch with the landlord, Sri. He was genuinely upset over what happened and wanted to remedy the problem immediately. Sri's a laid-back guy, around forty, and a native of India who grew up in California.

Sri immediately put us up in one of his other apartments, and it was out of *MTV Cribs*: four bedrooms, flat-screen televisions, leather couches, and a porch with a view of half of San Francisco. The bathroom was the size of my living room in the Netherlands.

Sri did whatever he could to make us comfortable. I came back to San Francisco a couple of months later, and he put me up in another apartment for free. We soon became great friends. We would hang out together. I'd eat dinner with him and his family. This may not seem unusual to you, but up until this stage in my life, nearly all my friendships had been forged out of business connections, and again, most of them were transactional: I do this for you, so you'll do that for me.

One day, I went to Sri's daughter's birthday party. It was a picnic in the Marina District in a park with a view of the Golden Gate Bridge. Sri's Indian and his wife is Chinese. They had a banquet set out on three benches. On one bench was traditional Chinese food, on another traditional Indian food, and on the last, all this salty, fatty American food. But it worked together perfectly. I felt free looking at everyone celebrating and enjoying the food. I thought about how you can blend all these cultures together, and it works. I started to ask myself again, *How could I be less biased by my own culture's me-first attitude so I could improve both my quality of life and that of everyone I encounter?*

When I mentor entrepreneurs today, the most successful ones learn that it's not the job of your coworkers, your employees, or your business partner to reward you for all the great things you do for them. The reward is seeing them thrive. It's a whole other way of doing business. I've seen massive acceleration in what entrepreneurs are able to accomplish when they make this shift.

As I traveled the world, I also learned not to take myself so seriously. Before, I was a perfectionist. Before, I didn't have competitors; I had enemies, and I wanted to destroy those enemies. I was famous for getting suppliers to cry over the phone as I bullied them for the lowest prices and for deals that had to be better than everyone else's. Today, I still know how to negotiate, but I don't need to demoralize and degrade people. My definition of success is different. If I use those tactics, I'm no longer a successful entrepreneur.

So what does make a successful entrepreneur? For starters, I discovered what I call the Entrepreneur's Pyramid. The ones at the top are those who succeed in a sustainable way by instinctively using the Five Facets. These entrepreneurs are the rock stars, the TED Talkers, the people living their destiny with successful ventures and helping other people do the same. At the bottom are the dreamers, the "wantrapreneurs" who never really go out, start a business, and make it succeed. Contrary to popular opinion, the bottom of the pyramid is important because that's where a lot of creativity and new ideas are incubating and buzzing around. In the second layer of the pyramid are entrepreneurs who are making and selling real businesses, but they need help getting to the next level. All the layers need one another, and my contribution is to keep knowledge flowing through each one. I'll talk more about some of the challenges inherent in the Entrepreneur's Pyramid in the next chapter.

CHAPTER TWO

THE ENTREPRENEUR'S PYRAMID

NICKY ROMERO IS ONE of the top DJs and music producers in the world. The Netherlands native has more than six million followers on Facebook and more than two million on Twitter. For years, Romero has been at the top of his game with his music label Protocol Recordings and related ventures. Then, seemingly out of the blue for fans, Romero's production slowed. Everyone wondered what was going on. At the end of 2015, Romero posted a personal message on Facebook to his followers that the reason he hadn't been releasing as much music as they wanted was because of anxiety. He had been dealing with severe anxiety for two and a half years, Romero wrote, and had seen more than twelve different therapists and professionals. He had a handle on it now, Romero continued, but had "felt guilty to all my fans, and more pressure was added by all [the] expectations."

Romero is at the top of the Entrepreneur's Pyramid; he is one of the heroes everyone looks up to. But occupying the top of the pyramid, being one of the richest and most visible people in your field, doesn't translate into fulfillment. Prioritizing success can wreck your well-being. As you know by now, that's what happened to me.

The biggest fallacy about the top of the Entrepreneur's Pyramid is that you have to kill yourself to get there. It's almost a mantra in Western culture. Sure, phases occur in your life when you have to work hard, such as the first and even second year of a start-up. But being in a state of permanent stress isn't sustainable. Permanent stress changes how your nervous system behaves; it alters the way your neurons fire. It's critical that you don't use overwork or perpetual busyness as a status symbol. To become a sustainable entrepreneur, that's not necessarily easy, but it is essential.

At the bottom of the pyramid is another fallacy. Would-be entrepreneurs located here always believe that the *idea* is paramount.

People come up to me all the time after my talks and say, "I've got this great idea."

Oh, no, not again, I think to myself.

It might be a football player who says, "Hey, my teammates

are always late, so I think having an app where the whole team can communicate all their dates and times with one another would be great. The person who's always late is going to have to buy beer for everyone else, and that's the thing that's going to make everyone want to buy our app."

"OK, great," I'll reply. "Who is going to make the app?"

Silence.

"Who is going to help you be successful?"

Silence.

"When are you going to start your business?"

More silence.

Now, when someone else comes up to me after a talk and says instead, "Hey, you know, I want to change my life and be independent from my employer. Even though I've never made an app before, I love programming. I'm a huge football fan, and if you're available to help me, I want to try and build an app myself that would help football teams in amateur leagues perform better."

That's someone who has a more well-balanced view on entrepreneurship.

Again, an idea alone is never enough to launch a business. You must also think about how to build an infrastructure around it. Otherwise, it's magical thinking. Focus on all the support you'll need personally and professionally to create a business first. What I see happening over and over again is people trying to sell themselves on one idea that isn't strong enough.

At a start-up weekend, I coached a young woman who worked at a bank. Laura wanted to leave her job because she had the idea of creating an app that would aggregate and analyze social media in order to assess global threats and risk patterns such as terrorism, extreme weather events, and stock market falls. At the end of the weekend, Laura learned that the idea wasn't entirely workable, but she was excellent at programming. Three years later, she has her own company making apps for other people. She has more business than she can handle. What she did was look at herself, learned what she loves doing and what she's good at, and created a career from that. She didn't become attached to a single idea and then put everything in her life behind it, potentially sacrificing her well-being and her finances.

Most people in the middle of the pyramid find it hard to move to the next level and get to the point where they're not doing all the work themselves. Building a team and creating the right DNA for the business is challenging. The first thing I do is help them build a network of mentors, which I will talk about later on.

Let's go back to the top of the pyramid. The entrepreneurs succeeding up here are using the Five Facets of Sustainable Entrepreneurship, which I will discuss in depth in the next section of this book. In brief, they are as follows:

1. The Idea
2. The Team
3. Planning
4. Resources
5. Health

Entrepreneurs might first approach the Five Facets as a model, but they soon discover it's a way of life. Every facet is interdependent with one another, and they shift in priority according to the needs of the moment. For example, during the initial phase of a start-up, the Resources facet is critical because money is one of your most important resources. When you land those finances, you'll often turn the focus toward the Team facet because you need to hire great people to execute at the highest level. But for a third-generation family business, money might not be an issue, but building an innovative team spirit might be critical.

You always have to push back when you find yourself focusing too much time on one facet.

No matter what your business is, imitating someone else isn't going to work. There's going to be only one Bill Gates and one Mark Zuckerberg. Steve Jobs didn't design Apple based on looking outside himself. He just had an internal drive combined with the weird combo of being a perfectionist, a business guy, and a spiritual seeker/hippie. From that, Jobs cooked up a billion-dollar enterprise. Look at yourself and find out how you want to live your life. Then design your business around that.

Toon van Veelen is a Dutch entrepreneur who runs an e-commerce business called ToneControl that sells professional DJ and producer gear. I've been his mentor for a while. In May 2016, *Sprout*, a Dutch magazine for entrepreneurs, interviewed him about the impact of our work together.

"From the first meeting, Sebastiaan made me think about what I was doing and why," said van Veelen in the piece. "Before that, I was guided by issues of the day, my mailbox—I had no planning, and it felt like I was making impulsive decisions all day. Through conversations with Sebastiaan, I took more time to think about his model and how to balance everything. I took a better look at my team: Who fits here and not there. For the first time in my life, I planned. Since Sebastiaan has been my mentor, ToneControl is growing much faster. Last year, we grew by 50 percent. But more important to me is that I now feel more relaxed and confident, and I'm able to make easier and better choices."

If you're not aware of the Five Facets, the tendency is to just react every day to what happens. You never take time to reflect and gain the helicopter view.

One of the ways out of this loop is to think about being the CEO not of your company but of your life. Then assess how you're doing and what advice you would give yourself from that perspective. Some of the common insights from people I've mentored include the following:

> "I see I don't have great people around me. I need a better team."

> "I haven't really thought about where I want my business to go. I'm on a circuitous route without a clear destination."

> "I've been struggling for years running this brick-and-mortar business, and I see the location isn't conducive to the appropriate customers finding me."

> "I've reached a high level of success, but I've lost control over my eating. I'm obese, and that's why I'm unhappy."

Eating out too much and getting fat might seem like a first-world problem, but it signifies a deeper rupture in the fabric of your life. Health is the most important facet. Without that, forget about everything else.

Now we'll look at how to use the Five Facets. I've found people do best when they choose the order in which they'll work through them. But I will say that for many people, health is a forgotten facet, and by prioritizing it, the other facets tend to fall into place. But by the time you finish this book, you'll be prepared to use the entire model to either solve your existing challenges as an entrepreneur or launch yourself into a life and career that works for you on all levels.

PART TWO

THE FIVE FACETS OF
SUSTAINABLE ENTREPRENEURSHIP

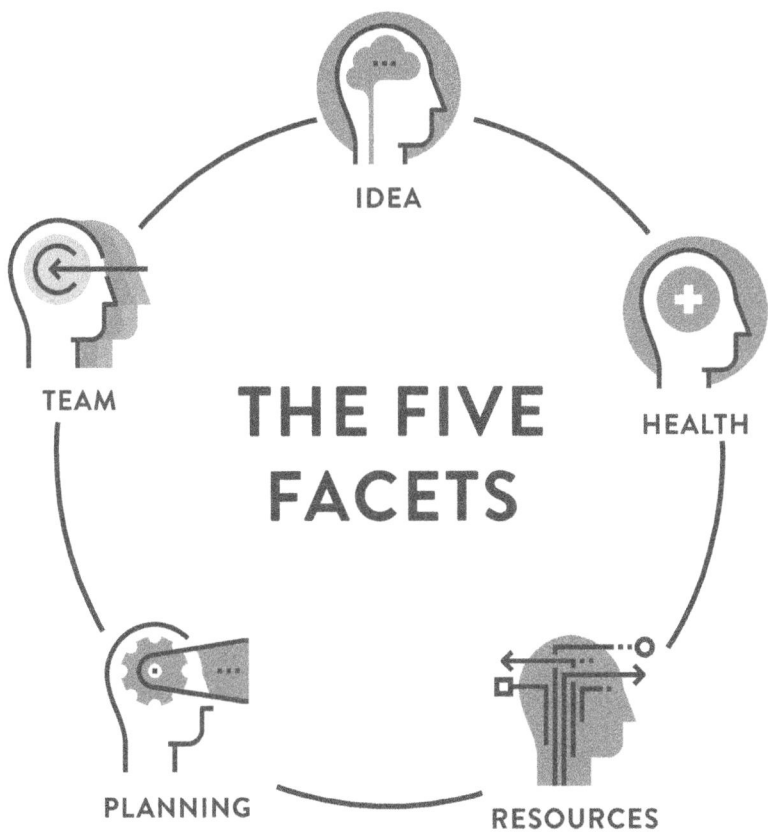

IDEA

HEALTH

THE FIVE FACETS

TEAM

PLANNING

RESOURCES

CHAPTER THREE
FIRST FACET: IDEA

GOLD AND PLATINUM RECORDS hung from the walls in the plush office. Fashionably dressed employees glided through the halls, discussing social media strategies and bookings for their multimillion-dollar clients. I was on sacred ground for musicians.

It's a little bit of a spoiler for readers of this book, but today, a big part of my life is centered on being an international DJ. As you may remember, I started my own record label of sorts when I was only fourteen years old. When I began redesigning my life after leaving the hospital, I realized music was my passion. I began practicing my DJ skills, developing my musicality, and most importantly, applying the Five Facets of Sustainable Entrepreneurship to my new career.

I made an appointment with Joeri Lodders, who runs a high-level management agency for artists in the Netherlands. One of their most famous artists is a Dutch music producer named Ferry Corsten who has worked with everyone from Justin Bieber and Public Enemy to The Killers and Nelly Furtado. Numerous records hanging on the agency's walls were Ferry's work. Being in Joeri's office, the seat of music royalty, was a little intimidating. I had gotten an appointment with Joeri through friends and colleagues I'd met in the music industry, and Joeri was already aware of my background as an entrepreneur.

He took me into a large meeting room, sat me down, and said, "Sebastiaan, thanks for dropping by. What can I do for you?"

"Joeri, you know I've been learning how to be a DJ for the past couple of months," I responded. "I've given it a lot of thought, and I've decided I'm going to go professional."

Joeri started laughing uncontrollably and didn't stop for five minutes. He laughed so hard he cried. Finally, he dried his tears and got ahold of himself.

"Sebastiaan, you have everything against you," he said. "It's a really bad idea to go out and be a professional DJ at age forty with almost no experience."

Then he gave me an appraising look. After a few moments, he shook his head ruefully.

"But you know what?" he said. "I'm going to help you. Because with all the support and resources you have around you, I believe you're going to make it."

So from day one in my new career, I've had one of the top managers in the business as one of my mentors. Why? Not because I had this great idea of being an international DJ, but because I had the entire infrastructure around me to make it happen.

Here's another example: Uber launched as a taxi app during a time when there were already hundreds of developers working on taxi apps. But from the start, it was clear Uber was going to be a market leader because it had the strongest investors and a top-notch team. Ideas come and go. To work, they have to be planted in the best soil and tended to by people who know how to apply the Five Facets. That's the key to this first facet.

The other mistake entrepreneurs make around their ideas is thinking they have to protect their uniqueness and keep them secret. Many people contact me for mentorship but then inform me that we can't work together until I sign a nondisclosure agreement (NDA) around the idea for their new venture. I always respond with, "OK, great. Let's make a deal. I'll sign the NDA, you tell me your idea, and if someone has already approached me with a similar idea, you'll pay me one hundred thousand dollars." No one ever makes me sign an NDA.

The reason is what's called the law of simultaneous invention, when multiple people have the same ideas around the world. As journalist Derek Thompson points out in a 2012 *Atlantic* article, inventions such as the lightbulb, cotton gin, and telegraph were not invented by one person. Thompson quotes Mark A. Lemley from a 2011 Stanford Law School paper that Lemley wrote called "The Myth of the Sole Inventor": "Simultaneous invention and incremental improvement are the way innovation works, even for radical inventions."

It would have been crazy for Elon Musk to run around and say to investors, "I'm going to design a car that's run on electricity, not gas, and I want you to sign this NDA." The first electric car made in the United States was introduced more than one hundred years ago. Sure, it could go only fourteen miles an hour and was more of an electric wagon, but still. Musk wasn't the first.

Paul Graham, cofounder of start-up incubator Y Combinator, has said on his blog, "Because a good idea should seem obvious, when you have one you'll tend to feel that you're late. Don't let that deter you. Worrying that you're late is one of the signs of a good idea. Ten minutes of searching the Web will usually settle the question. Even if you find someone else working on the same thing, you're probably not too late. It's exceptionally rare for start-ups to be killed by competitors—so rare that you can almost discount the possibility. So unless you discover a competitor with the sort of lock-in that would prevent users from choosing you, don't discard the idea."

I meet so many people who come up with an idea for a product or service, go into their basement and lock the door, and then work for weeks and months refining it. Then when everything has been made to perfection, they emerge and present their gift to the world. But it turns out that no one is interested because while they were sequestered, the world changed, and what they have to offer nobody needs anymore. Can you think of anything more horrible for an entrepreneur? Please let me save you from this fate.

For example, Malcolm Gladwell describes in a 2004 *New Yorker* article how in the 1980s, Campbell's was striving to create a spaghetti sauce with their Prego brand that rivaled Ragú. "At Ragú and Prego, they had been striving for the platonic spaghetti sauce, and the platonic spaghetti sauce was thin and blended because that's the way they thought it was done in Italy," Gladwell writes. But market researcher Howard Moscowitz discovered after extensive testing and interviewing that a whole new category was needed: extra chunky. "Over the next decade, that new category proved to be worth hundreds of millions of dollars to Prego," writes Gladwell.

My advice to every entrepreneur is to do your homework and be transparent about your ideas. The more open you are about what you're up to, the better people are able to help you succeed or participate.

Take Nike. The company regularly publishes a public calendar on its website of when it's going to be releasing new tennis shoes, sneakers, and other gear. If I'm Adidas or Puma, I can read the schedule and launch a better-priced competitor in any category the same week. But Nike is so powerful and strong that it's confident it can hold its own no matter what its competitors are doing.

In my new career as a DJ, for example, I put everything I'm doing online on my website, such as the road map of the projects I'm going to release plus all my strategies. Everything is right out there for my competitors to see. Giving out all this information does two things.

First, it strengthens my position in the public as a thought leader. Second, it has a psychological effect on me, impacting how I think about myself and talk to myself. My internal dialogue goes something along the lines of, *What I'm doing is coming from a place of contribution, so I don't worry about competition. My goal is to learn, to grow, and be an influencer of positive regard.*

So please remember, ideas whose time has come happen all the time, and transparency around your own ideas is always the place of power.

CHAPTER FOUR
SECOND FACET: TEAM

BY NOW, YOU KNOW THE IMPORTANCE of focusing on what you like doing and what you're good at in order to not crash and burn. But everyone has weaknesses. You need a great team to scale the heights of the Entrepreneur's Pyramid. But that team, which is the second facet, has multiple layers.

Whenever I say that you need a great team, most people think I'm talking from the get-go about the employees you hire or the professional advisers you pay. I'm not.

What's required in the very beginning, right there at base camp when you're either conceptualizing or forming your venture, is a team of mentors. This is a group of experts you don't pay and who are willing to answer your questions about your strategies and tactics to grow.

You should never try to ascend the pyramid by yourself. An experienced trekker would rarely ever climb a mountain alone in real life, and you shouldn't attempt to do so in entrepreneurship.

It's critical to define the areas where you need expertise. When I decided to become an international DJ, I asked myself questions such as "Where can I learn how to DJ professionally?" "How do I build a digital content strategy?" "What gear do I need, and how do I build a studio at home?" "How do I obtain bookings and clients?" Then I set out to find mentors who could advise me on those areas, such as Joeri Lodders at the top management agency for artists I discussed in the last chapter. Bottom line: The purpose of a team of mentors is to solve specific gaps in your knowledge.

I teach people to be extremely selective when it comes to choosing your team of mentors. For example, if you're starting a brick-and-mortar store, you need to be in a prime location. You'll need a retail expert to help you define where that is. You could research the top five real estate businesses in your area, see who founded them, and find out which founder might be semi-retired but still connected and involved in the industry and willing to mentor you. Dig deep and get creative in your quest.

In my experience, most people underestimate how willing prospective mentors will be to help you. The higher in the hierarchy the people you approach are, the more they remember what it was like when they were first starting out and how much they needed help.

Use LinkedIn, Twitter, and other social media routes to

contact potential mentors. Ask friends and connections to make an introduction for you. One way of asking for mentorship is, "Listen, I'm creating a superior team of mentors to help me grow as an entrepreneur and a person. I would appreciate fifteen to thirty minutes of your time to ask you one or two questions. Then I'd also like to ask a third question and that is, 'What can I do for you?'"

One of the most valuable things you can do for your mentors is to connect them with one another. For example, I've created a WhatsApp group on my phone to which all my mentors belong. Of course, I use the group to ask questions and provide updates on my progress. It also provides the opportunity for them to meet and contribute to one another. They have found that invaluable. The best mentors are consistently seeking to grow personally and professionally themselves in new areas, so they often need mentoring as well.

It probably goes without saying, but you must always treat your mentors with care. Do everything possible to appreciate them. In our interactions, I treat my mentors with first-date behavior: I'm nervous, serious, and doing everything I can to please them.

Many entrepreneurs are loners. I was for fifteen years. You've got to fight back against this tendency and see it as unnatural rather than natural.

TWO TEAMS COME NEXT

When you have traction with your team of mentors and your business is up and running, the next team you need is professional: a lawyer, a business manager, and an accountant. Often, people see a lawyer as someone who puts out fires. I'd like you to view your lawyer as someone who helps you build your business, and I advise asking her/him specific ways s/he believes s/he can help you do so. A great lawyer, for example, can help generate royalties, as DJ Nicky Romero's lawyer does.

Most lawyers either represent other entrepreneurs or see themselves as entrepreneurs, too. It's important to find a lawyer who gives you the feeling that your business is secure in his/her hands. You'd be surprised at how financially literate lawyers turn out to be and how much they speak the language of business. Most important, they understand the difference between things like gross margin, profit, and revenue and are able to create legal processes that touch the very core of your financial health. Take my legal adviser, Harro. He works for one of the largest and most traditional firms in the world, and his hourly rate is super high. Nevertheless, Harro takes the time to go out for coffee with me regularly. He doesn't charge me anything. Nearly every time, I come back with solid leads (mostly his other clients) and new insight on how to build my mentorship and speaking practice. The reason he wants to do coffee is not only because I know the best coffee places in town, but also because his law firm is looking to adopt a more service-oriented model, and I'm asking him the right questions.

The next stage and third team that is required is comprised of your employees. Most people starting out have an employee team made up of what's called friends, family, and fools. Take a family restaurant, for example. Mom will be out front taking orders, Dad is in the back cooking, and the kids are doing the dishes. Friends are doing promotion and marketing in their off hours. Maybe you bartered with some acquaintances for social media help. Unfortunately, it's hard to excel over time with this group of employees. When you realize you're depending on a team of friends, family, and fools, it's time to hire the best outsiders you can based on their expertise, if, of course, you have the financial resources to do so.

Entrepreneurs don't realize that the first hires you make are always the most important ones. You always want to hire people aligned with your vision. In a Stanford talk, Airbnb cofounder and CEO Brian Chesky said he "ran through thousands of applicants and interviewed hundreds of people" when looking for his first employee, according to the blog *Kissmetrics*. After six months, he found lead engineer Nick Grandy. *Kissmetrics* quotes Chesky: "Somebody asked me, 'What's the job of a CEO?' and there's a number of things a CEO does. What you mostly do is articulate the vision, develop the strategy, and you gotta hire people to fit the culture. If you do those three things, you basically have a company. And that company will hopefully be successful, if you have the right vision, the right strategy, and good people."

I remember one of the first employees we hired at the micro roastery. Marcel walked into our place, looked around, and an amazed look crossed his face. Our roastery was the Apple store of coffee beans: white, clean, modern, high-tech, and super friendly. "Wow," he said as he shook my hand, "I love your environment!"

Marcel was a sales guy for magazine advertorials, which hardly anyone advertises in anymore. His company had tanked, and he had lost his job. On a deeper level, he hadn't seen the signs of impending doom and had neglected to redesign his life in time. During his job interview with us, we found out he didn't even drink coffee. But we could see that not only was he a great salesperson because of the way he sold himself to us, but he also matched our culture because of his appreciation for our environment. I hired him on the spot, and within one month, our revenue was 600 percent higher.

One of the mistakes entrepreneurs make is to try and save money by hiring interns or people who need a great deal of training. This will end up being the blind leading the blind. It's always great to have a few interns running around bringing that fresh, alive energy to your venture, but the best thing is to hire the most experienced, senior people you can find. Be open to how you find them, especially serendipitous routes. One day, a regular at our coffee roastery mentioned to me, "Hey, my boyfriend worked at a coffee company until about a year ago." I didn't think too much of it until the guy stopped in for an espresso a week or so later. It turns out he was the former CEO of Douwe Egberts, one of the largest coffee roasters in the world. He joined our team a couple of weeks later and introduced us to a higher level of roasting beans than we ever could have imagined.

Maintaining your focus over time on hiring great people is essential. One of the companies I invested in was a made-to-measure suit company. The guy who founded it was one of the best tailors in the Netherlands. But he lost his hiring focus and ended up bringing on tailors who weren't as skilled as he was. All his customers were used to his level of quality and service, and they ended up being disappointed when they didn't receive it from someone else. Clients would say to him, "OK, I'll see the tailor you assign me, but I'd like to stop by your office later in the week and have you double-check how s/he did the work." When you have to sell hundreds of suits a month, and they all end up going through your own hands, that's not a viable business model. The founder never ended up being able to grow his business.

Meanwhile, having a large number of employees was once a status symbol for tech start-ups. Today, it's the other way around. If you go to your typical restaurant around the corner, it might employ more people, between chefs and waitstaff, than your average start-up right now. For example, photo-sharing site Instagram had thirteen employees when it was bought by Facebook for $1 billion in spring 2012. A couple of years later, Facebook gobbled up WhatsApp for $16 billion; the messenger app start-up had only thirty-five engineers and was reaching 450 million users. In 2015, WeTransfer raised $25 million in new funding to expand in the United States, Europe, and internationally. At that time, the four-year-old company—with 25 million active users sending 70 million files per month—had approximately thirty staff members and had been profitable since 2013. It's not only tech start-ups that have recognized that fewer employees is good business. Pepsi sells syrup to bottlers who do all the rest: adding the sugar, water, and carbonation, as well as performing all the bottling and distribution. A former Pepsi employee told me that at headquarters, an oft-told joke is that only two people are required to work at the automated syrup-manufacturing plant: one to sweep the floors and the other to count the money.

Don't ever think that the success of your business is measured by having a large staff. The bigger question to ask is, "How much revenue are we bringing in per employee?"

HIRING IS DATING

In addition, the hiring paradigm has changed for tech employers. Knowledge workers today are fluid: This year, they might be working at Google, next year at Facebook or another start-up where their expertise is needed and valued. The concept of "owning" your employees doesn't exist anymore. The most successful employers today focus on the shared goals they have with their employees and how they can provide a platform where employees can do great work and increase their quality of life. That's why the hiring process is so critical because when you find the right match, you'll experience less turnover, superior work, and ultimately, more revenue. Most employers still focus solely on getting stuff out of people.

The answer is to treat the hiring process, across the board, like dating. In ancient times (ancient by start-up standards but in reality, a decade ago), after being screened by Human Resources, you would arrive for a job interview and be passed up the ladder from person to person, all the while having static conversations with the same set of rules. Today, employers and prospective employees have to practice the art of falling in love and seducing each other.

On a first meeting (a.k.a. first date), that's the time to share information and see if there's a spark. The next step is to move into doing stuff together. For example, if you're hiring someone to design products for you, ask him/her to participate in a product-design session. During that session, evaluate how candidates behave and interact with your staff. You can test out and refine your dating/hiring process with interns and temporary employees at first. But as Eric Schmidt and Jonathan Rosenberg put it in their book *How Google Works* (Hachette, 2014), "Scouting [talent] is like shaving. If you don't do it every day, it shows." For fast-growing companies, sometimes 50 percent of your daily time must be spent finding the right employees.

So to extend the dating metaphor, you want that feeling with the prospective employee of "I want to spend time with this person." By doing stuff together—eating a meal, having coffee, working on a short-term project, and so on—you can discover whether you have matching values. I encourage even doing more activities that aren't work-related, such as taking a hike together on the weekend. You'll start to see each other for the people you are, without the rose-colored glasses, and know whether you have a good foundation for a long-term working relationship. A salesperson with a materialistic nature, for example, is just not going to be a great fit in a social venture. From a management perspective, revenue might grow and profit increase, but the culture will be polluted, creating a negative impact.

Most people skip the dating step and end up needing to divorce bad hires. Others find love at first sight but don't know how to build a sustainable relationship for the long term. A CEO

I mentored hired everyone for his company based solely on looking at their résumé. He didn't check with former clients or employers. The salespeople he hired were a disaster. On paper, it looked like they had generated great sales, but most of them came from an environment where they never had to come up with their own leads. They didn't know how to get out there and make things happen on their own. When it comes to hiring, due diligence works.

THE MAN (OR WOMAN) IN THE MIRROR

Stasis occurs in every marriage and in every company. Several years ago, I mentored three entrepreneurs. They were investing in start-ups, and when I asked why, the answer was that they were bored with their own Internet services company that built and maintained websites.

"We're making a lot of money," one of the guys told me in a meeting. "Everyone seems happy. But every day now when I go to work, I don't see any challenge in running the thing anymore."

I looked hard at the three of them.

"Are you sure everyone's happy?" I asked them. "If I was one of your employees, and you're giving me the signal every day at work that you're bored, how do you think that's going to make me feel?"

"Bored," the three replied in unison.

"Why don't you take all this excitement and energy you have

around investing in Internet start-ups and bring it to your own company and your own employees?" I asked them.

When you stop putting energy into your ventures, your team will notice it. Their own excitement and commitment will wither and die like tulips in summer. The great people will leave, and the ones who stay will be bored, just like you. Eventually, you'll kill the culture in your once-thriving business, no matter how much money you make. You've been in workplaces like that. Everyone's watching the clock or their backs. These guys were midcareer and thought they'd seen it all. But when they turned their attention back to their employees, they regained their spark, and their employees did, too. Extreme revenue growth followed. One of the simple things they did was redesign the office pantry and turn it into a coffee bar. It changed the energy of the workplace from flat to dynamic.

It wasn't the remodel per se that changed the energy; it was the attention given to the employees. How this phenomenon, called the Hawthorne effect, was first identified is described in a 2008 article in *The Economist* online. The Hawthorne effect is based on "one of the most famous experiments...in industrial history," which took place in the late 1920s and 1930s at a Western Electric plant in Hawthorne, a suburb outside Chicago. The experiments were originally conceived to boost productivity. At first, one group of employees' lighting was changed; the other was not. Productivity rose in the group with better lighting. Then other changes were implemented such as hours and breaks, "and in all cases their productivity improved when a change was made." But when everything went back to how it was in the first place, productivity was still high. "The experimenters concluded," notes *The Economist*, "that it was not the changes in physical conditions that were affecting the workers' productivity. Rather, it was the fact that someone was actually concerned about their workplace, and the opportunities this gave them to discuss changes before they took place."

Start-ups today understand the importance of bestowing attention on their employees. While researching this book, I visited Dropbox's new offices. In one of the meeting rooms, they had installed a full recording studio, complete with instruments anyone could use. You could literally record a professional album there. They thought it would be fun for employees to have that option. As an employer, you don't have to go that extreme or others—like Apple paying for female employees to freeze their eggs to safeguard their fertility—but you can do smaller things, from meditation classes to on-site massages for tired shoulders. What motivates people is your attention and your care.

Happiness incentives are another option that often proves successful. One example is Google's 20-percent time, which is the free time during which employees can work on promising side projects. In the Netherlands, ABN AMRO, one of the largest banks in my country, installed beehives on the roof that employees can help maintain. The honey harvested is used in the corporate restaurant. Meanwhile, at KLM airlines, employees can apply to be part of the professional deicing team for aircraft. You might be looking out the window of your plane readying for takeoff, and one of the workers in those orange vests deicing your Boeing 747 is the head of Human Resources.

In the end, your team is a living, breathing organism. Just like you wouldn't thrive during an operation without the right donor for your blood type, your team won't thrive without a good match in the employees you hire. Neglecting your team destroys the health of your business and your mental well-being.

Entrepreneurs on the road to burnout can never lead a team to the highest level. I always advise flailing super(wo)men to take on a second responsibility in their lives that doesn't have anything to do with the business they're running, such as getting involved in a charity. It helps break the cycle of people working harder and harder yet becoming more inefficient. They usually get advice like go to the gym more or get a hobby, but that doesn't address a deeper unrest. The incentives in working for a charity are different than working for your own company. Through being a charity's board member, fund raiser, or adviser, you find out there's more to life than increasing the value of your business for your own ego. You also meet other strong personalities who confront you without the tension of their being your employees or team members.

FOUNDER BREAKUPS

The wrong team isn't the main reason start-ups fail. Founder breakups are the primary problem. These breakups can be traced back to failing to go through the dating process correctly. I made this error with a company I cofounded that imported musical instruments into the United States. My cofounder and I were infatuated with the idea and rushed into it, but I found out six months later how different we were. I projected my capacity as a sales guy onto him and thought he knew how to cold call, how to take the initiative to show up at music stores and give demos, and how to generate leads and conduct presentations. But he didn't have a clue.

If we'd dated long enough, I would have discovered that he lacked those skills, including that he didn't even possess a car to make it to meetings.

Founder breakups are an inevitable part of start-up life, so they're not necessarily a bad thing. Once you know you're not on the same page anymore, though, there's a reluctance to initiate and then go through the awkward and painful process of breaking up. But every day you wait makes it more difficult. Break up as fast and cleanly as you can, especially before the lawyers get involved.

CHAPTER FIVE
THIRD FACET: PLANNING

YOU THINK WHEN YOU'RE THE BOSS, people would read your e-mails, right? Not necessarily. I was in the elevator with one of the employees at a start-up I ran. I proudly mentioned an award the company had recently won and how it had accelerated our business.

"What award?" the employee said.

"It was in the staff-wide e-mail," I replied.

A guilty look crossed his face. Silence. Thankfully for him, the elevator chimed and the door opened.

I'd been sending e-mails for months to my employees, detailing our wins and accolades, as well as our staff promotions, with the goal of motivating people. But inspiring your people is an art, not a science, something that cannot be forced any more than you can make people stop watching cat videos on YouTube.

So I decided to hold a mini town hall meeting once a month and invite everyone who worked for me to come. The first time I organized it, nobody showed up. The excuses were things like, "I have to pick up my kids," or "I have a doctor's appointment and can't change it." So I made attendance mandatory.

At the second gathering, I talked about where we were going as a company. It may sound a little sappy, but I put my heart into everything I was saying.

I made a date for the third town hall meeting, but it turned out I had a new client in town. I sent out an e-mail saying I needed to cancel and was inundated with a barrage of e-mails from the staff. "You can't do that!" they said. "We need this event to continue!"

The third time of anything can be the charm. At the gathering, the staff was eager to know more about the future of our company.

"OK," I told them, "we're going to put ourselves on a time line. I'm going to talk about what happened last month, the goals we're setting today, and what we're going to do next month." I put every single person who worked for us on that time line, and I started moving them across it. What happened was that people not only felt more connected to what we were doing, but they also had a better understanding of the why.

People have an innate need to feel oriented in time and space. When you put yourself and your team on a time line, it's almost as if they see themselves as characters in a movie. They know the plot and feel secure knowing how it's going to unfold.

Great entrepreneurs are great planners. It used to be that every start-up had a business plan: Remember those unwieldy books describing your company? You'd have a marketing plan, financial projections, and so on. It may sound sacrilegious, but most start-up founders I know don't do that anymore. What they do instead is what I did with my staff at that third meeting: put themselves on a time line and then describe the challenges they're facing and how they're going to solve them, taking small incremental steps that are focused on learning what works as quickly as possible. They know that the sooner you make mistakes, the sooner you learn from them. (Think about the last big mistake you made. How much did it cost you? How much would it have been worth to you to have found out sooner that you were making the mistake?)

The best founders have a one-minute pitch of where they've been, where they are, and where they're going. That's the twenty-first-century way of planning.

When I mentor teams, I do an exercise where I interview each member one at a time without the other teammates present. I ask them to describe what it is their company does, and I record the interview. When I'm done, I play the recordings for the entire team. Say it's a team of six. When I play the six different recordings, it's like hearing about six different businesses. But with a time line, you get people on the same page at the same time.

My own time line is comprised of three levels: strategic, tactical, and operational. Strategic plans are made twice a year. (I do mine, for your information, after taking long walks.) Tactical planning is done once a month. Basically, I'm redesigning my tactics by listening, learning, and adapting. Operational planning is done daily. I don't plan every second of my day, but I have some idea of what the results should be at the end of it and how I'm balancing my time. I also make appointments with mentors who are experts in the specific areas in which I am making plans. For example, one of my mentors is an expert in digital content. Each month, we meet up and discuss where I am on the specific time line we've created that's designed to push me into the next phase of increasing my capabilities. We work to solve every issue that prohibits me from moving to the next phase in the time line.

There's an inspirational saying for business: "Great drivers are always looking in the rearview mirror." It's the type of thing you see as a framed print in a SkyMall catalog. I don't agree when it comes to time lines. Above all, the most important thing is that entrepreneurs know where they are going.

TRANSPARENT PLANNING

The other day, I had a meeting with a start-up I'm mentoring that's the Uber of private jets. It designs the technology to know where the jets are at any given time in each airport, their capacity, availability, and related aspects. One of the issues it's facing is that a key investor negotiated a strong role in the decision-making process with the founder and his team. As a result, progress has slowed, and the start-up has become more indecisive because the investor isn't working there on a daily basis. All these microdecisions have to go through him.

In short, the jet-sharing founders weren't clear in their communication with the investor from the start on what their time line was and the precedence of their vision. They also weren't transparent along the way with him about what they needed, why, and when.

Start-ups often give away too much independence to bring in funding. They go through tough negotiations to get needed cash, but those negotiations can push them in a direction that may not serve them as entrepreneurs. They end up trying to please their investors too much.

Go for mutuality with your investors: "both/and" solutions not "either/or" ones. Start communicating your goals at an early phase and stick with them. Make it clear to your investors that they are investing in a team, and that team has a vision.

This is even more critical now because of the time compression in entrepreneurship. In the early days, you would start a business for the long haul. All the decisions you made were about planting seeds for a future way down the road. Today, entrepreneurs are thinking about the eventual sale of the company from the moment they conceptualize the business. In 1995, the start-to-sale time for a company was twenty years; today, it's fifteen; by 2020, it will be seven. The importance of a time line takes on an extra dimension if you're making decisions based on selling a company in seven years. You've got shorter runways and less margin for error. Your identity and ego can't be tied so closely to the business either.

HEADING FOR THE DOOR

How do you know when it's time to leave or sell your company? You must ask yourself two questions. (This applies to entrepreneurs seeking to grow as individuals. Many people have other, important reasons to stay, sell, or leave.)

1. Can we still grow in this market?
2. Is there an opportunity to be number one in the market?

If you solve both problems, there's no opportunity for growth, and it's time to sell. I mentored an entrepreneur who ran a start-up that sold tablets and smartphones. His business had the opportunity to grow aggressively and become number one. But even though he was the owner of the company, he simply did not want to be the leader. He made plans to depart and hired a director to run things. But the team never accepted the director; everyone wanted the owner to stay. It wasn't the time for him to leave. On the flip side, I mentored a couple of entrepreneurs who ran an Internet retailer. They had no chance of becoming number one. They didn't know how to aggressively grow the company. When they had the opportunity to sell, they took it, and it was the right move.

MAKING THINGS VISIBLE

Yes, we're talking about transparency again. It's one of the mantras of this book. If you're not communicating your business model to others, people can't get involved. I always recommend that companies have a big whiteboard in their office space that displays their business model. Not only will employees see it every day, so will visitors to your office.

For example, when you're not generating enough revenue, take a chance and invite visitors to help solve the problem by writing their ideas on the whiteboard. (Another excellent tool is entrepreneur Alex Osterwalder's Business Model Canvas, found at strategyzer.com. It's a one-page template designed to simplify problem solving within business models.) You'd be surprised at how many brilliant, smart people visit your offices every day and would love to help you. But if you're attached to keeping up appearances and telling everyone that everything's going well when it's not, you're not allowing people to help you.

Keeping up appearances is a self-made booby trap. The strongest entrepreneurs are the first ones to admit where they fail, where they're insecure, and where they need help. You never know your positive impact on others by being open and real.

For example, when I was in the hospital for my breakdown, I refused to wear a name tag because I didn't want anyone to put two and two together. I was terrified of being recognized. One morning, I picked up an old magazine in the lobby and saw an interview with me, and I ripped the article to pieces. For months, I was in denial. I'd say to myself something like, *I'm a profoundly successful celebrity entrepreneur. Hell, I have four Porsches at home, including a 911 Turbo, plus a Maserati. What the f**k am I doing here?*

Two years after my breakdown, the business magazine *Quote* approached me. If you'll remember, *Quote* is like the Dutch version of *Forbes*. *Quote* had found out about my breakdown and wanted to know if I'd permit them to interview me about it for a piece on the downside of wealth. *Quote* can be pretty nasty with their celebrity articles. I thought about it, swallowed hard, and told them I'd do it, and I'd trust them to tell my story with integrity. The interview was the first time in my life I had been completely transparent about something.

I was amazed by the outcome.

I received hundreds of e-mails from organizations and companies that wanted to book me as a motivational speaker, as well as many from former business partners praising me for my honesty. However, the best part was I received even more e-mails from people struggling with challenges on their own hero's journey who thanked me for inspiring them.

COMMUNICATION CREATES BUY-INS

Part of being transparent is being able to communicate effectively. I had a pivotal experience with one of our interns that made me realize how much I needed to improve in this arena. Sara worked in the marketing department of one of my companies. My mode of operation was always to give interns a great deal of responsibility, about as much as a regular employee. Sara was responsible and professional; you never needed to tell her anything twice. One day, she approached me and told me she was leaving the company.

"Why?" I asked.

"I'm quitting school," Sara replied.

"Listen," I said, "I don't want you to quit school, but if you're going to do that, let me hire you as one of our marketing associates."

"No, thank you," she said. "I'm going to go work as a barista at Starbucks." I was shocked and then puzzled.

"Why in the world would you leave a marketing job that's the start of an impressive career to go work in a green apron at a coffee bar?" I asked her.

"Because they *care*," she said cryptically.

I started researching Starbucks. Its mission is to create a culture that nurtures employees and imbues them with the goal of amazing their customers and providing a second home for them. The result is that even a barista feels like s/he can grow the company. That motivated me to build an amazing culture at my companies instead of only offering great jobs. I wanted people to want to work for me, not for the position.

THE POWER OF AN EVENTUAL-SALE MENTALITY

I've emphasized how planning is the ability to involve employees and others into your journey. That becomes even more valuable if you're starting a business that you'll eventually sell. If you communicate all along the way, right up until the point of sale, then nobody gets a nasty surprise.

When you're planning to sell a company, you must perform commercial and financial due diligence, prepare all your contracts for other parties to read, communicate to employees, and talk with accountants. It seems overwhelming at first. It reminds me of that saying, "How in the world do you eat an elephant?" Answer: "One bite at a time."

Because that process is so extensive, I've found that one of the most effective things entrepreneurs can do is run their company as if they are going to sell it, whether they do or not. You discover the amazing aspects of the company you've created and the areas you've neglected. With an eventual-sale mentality, you will always create a better business. In addition, you aren't so invested emotionally in its success or failure. Businesses come and go. But you have only one life, and it's not a test run.

I've mentored many CEOs who think they've been communicating with their employees about a potential sale, but the employees are clueless. It's similar to the way people act in long-term marriages: They somehow expect their spouse to have read their minds. Don't expect your employees to be mind readers or take on the job of figuring out what you're doing. It's not the role of your environment to keep track of you. It's your role as an entrepreneur to keep your environment current on what you're up to, as well as the state of the company.

In a different context, I saw the impact of poor communication when I mentored the staff of a nongovernmental organization (NGO). It was an environmental organization focusing on the Amazon rain forest (I've changed some identifying details to protect the organization's privacy). It wanted to learn how to raise venture capital because individual financial donations and governmental support were down. We discovered most of the people on the NGO's management side didn't know how much revenue the organization generated, how many staff members it had, and other key pieces of knowledge. The leaders also didn't seriously involve staff members lower on the totem pole, so those people were incentivized to stay in the dark.

I took the entire NGO through a process where they would come up with an entrepreneurial idea and go on a faux road show to pitch it to investors. They came up with a plan to create a space where tourists could observe wildlife and the rain forest without the environment being disturbed.

"We could have a restaurant there," proposed one staff member when it came to how to generate revenue.

"No, let's sell tickets instead," replied another.

They did the worst thing you can do: assume stuff without testing it. I gave them a five-hour presentation on how investors think, and two of the things they didn't realize was that (1) you have to have a business model and (2) an investor is not a bank. An investor wants to generate value; a bank wants to generate interest.

Bottom line: The board expected their staff to be entrepreneurial but didn't hire anyone with that background. For both the board and their staff, it was a case of "you don't know what you don't know."

NO SURPRISES

I'd like to circle back to the beginning of this chapter when I discussed the importance of having a time line. When you have a high level of transparency in your company or organization, all the team members are on the same page and buy in (not only team members but everyone around the organization such as investors, customers, business partners, suppliers, even the family members of all those people). The result is that your team will start pushing you across the time line instead of you having to push them.

That's the sweet spot as a leader.

But leaders forget the fundamental importance of actually telling your team the underlying motivation of *why* you want something. Here's an example that may seem inconsequential at first glance. Many entrepreneurs complain that the kitchen in their office is never clean. They always tell me how they have to clean it themselves.

"OK," I'll respond, "but how did you communicate to the staff that the kitchen should always be clean?"

"I made a list of the daily tasks, like you're responsible for unloading the dishwasher on this day," owners say.

"That's the wrong approach; that's a rule book," I say. "Nobody reads the rules, and nobody wants to be on a calendar where they have to do the dishes every Monday. What you have to do is discuss with your employees what kind of business you want to run and hire team members attracted to that kind of culture. When you walk into an Apple store, you know that the stuff you're buying is just as beautiful on the inside as it is on the outside. The people Apple hire have that mentality, too. The way a business looks is a reflection of how it operates. That's what you have to communicate."

In the end, if you want clean and crispy, you have to hire clean and crispy.

WHAT IT'S LIKE AT THE TOP

Returning to the Entrepreneur's Pyramid. The people at the pinnacle have learned that being open, helping other people, and sharing their knowledge results in their own growth and success.

As I mentioned before, in my twenties I worked at Gartner, the technology and research firm, giving C-level advice to companies on their strategies. I discovered that most people at the top were open about stuff that wasn't going well. They didn't have middle manager syndrome where they were trying to please the people above and kick down the people below. At the C level, people would tell me their worries and issues and permit me to help them. That's the reason people reach that level: They're able to identify the issues their enterprise faces and know how to inform others that those problems need to be solved.

If you're an executive or entrepreneur, you need to know everything about your company and your team. As far as a time line, you should know where you came from, where you're going, what you don't have, and what you need. Use all that information, and make sure you communicate it to everyone else—clearly and directly.

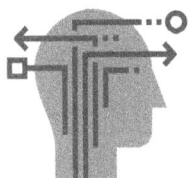

CHAPTER SIX

FOURTH FACET: RESOURCES

dreamer

noun

1. a person who dreams or is dreaming.

2. a person who is unpractical or idealistic.
"a rebellious young dreamer"
synonyms: fantasist, daydreamer, romantic, sentimentalist, idealist, wishful thinker, Don Quixote, utopian, visionary
"part of me will always be a dreamer"

doer

noun

1. the person who does something.
"the doer of the action"
synonyms: performer, perpetrator, executor, accomplisher, agent
"the doer of unspeakable deeds"

2. a person who acts rather than merely talking or thinking.
"I'm a doer, not a moaner"
synonyms: worker, organizer, man/woman of action

3. informal mover and shaker, busy bee.
"Daniel is a thinker more than a doer"

THIS IS HOW GOOGLE'S DICTIONARY defines dreamers and doers. But what actually separates the dreamers from the doers is that the dreamers have thought through the resources they will need to execute their vision. For example, starting a business that is based on selling users an app when you do not have any knowledge about how to make apps, and don't know anyone willing to help you, is just not workable. Think about it, people! Even if you have the money, finding someone these days who can build a great app is virtually impossible. These are the most sought-after people on the planet. I mentor would-be app entrepreneurs all the time who don't think about that one crucial fact.

Most entrepreneurs aren't aware that Resources, the fifth facet, are something you must manage on a daily basis. You not only have to make lists of what you don't have and a plan to obtain those resources, but you also have to *believe* you can find whatever it is you don't have. It's a gut-level feeling in your bones. To paraphrase the American automobile pioneer Henry Ford: There is no man or woman living who can do more than s/he thinks s/he can.

In chapter two ("The Entrepreneur's Pyramid"), I told you the story of Laura, the young woman I met at a start-up weekend. She worked at a bank but had the idea of creating an app that measured global threats and risk patterns by aggregating and analyzing social media. (The global risks include events like terrorism, extreme-weather events, major strikes, and stock market falls.)

She eventually decided the idea wouldn't work and became a successful app developer. But the actual reason Laura became an app developer in the first place was because while in pursuit of her idea, she identified that she needed the resource of knowing how to make apps.

TOP THREE RESOURCES

The most important resources for any entrepreneur are money, people, and time. Time is the Achilles' heel of your resources because time is not scalable. You have only twenty-four hours in a day. Time is your most precious investment in anything you do as an entrepreneur. You should always be tracking how much time you're putting into something and whether it is worth it.

No is a complete sentence. I'd like you to memorize what I just said and repeat after me: *No is a complete sentence.* Saying no is simply one of the most important things you have to learn as an entrepreneur. One of the main things that caused my burnout breakdown is that I almost never said no to anyone. I always said yes because I thought it was important as an entrepreneur to always be enthusiastic and jump on any idea that sounded good. But that resulted in my working seven days a week, eighteen hours a day, and not necessarily on things that were aligned with my passion and my vision.

Bottom line: I did not protect my time as an important resource. If you're having difficulties deciding whether to say "yes" or "no" to an idea or a business move that's already in place, here's a mind trick that I teach people. Just ask, "Has it helped or will it likely help to generate revenue this month?" If so, then the answer is yes.

So figuring out your most important resources will help you identify when to say no. Being aware is what I'm talking about. That way, you won't be saying no randomly. For example, if you're a novelist—and most novelists are entrepreneurs, believe it or not—a calm day may be an important resource for you in order to execute at the highest level. So your task is not to have calm days but to create them. Find out what it is you need to create those days; maybe it's doing fewer projects a month and cutting back in order to balance your revenue with your costs. Calmer days mean better writing, and better writing means better books.

When it comes to hiring the right people, very few entrepreneurs know more about how to do so than Keith Rabois. He played pivotal roles in building Silicon Valley companies like PayPal, LinkedIn, and Square. "You've got to find people who are undiscovered," he told journalist Kara Swisher in the podcast *Re/code Decode*. "That's the core ingredient for a CEO and a start-up, being able to find those people and assess them when the rest of the world doesn't know how to assess them yet."

THE MAGIC OF TEAMWORK AND FEEDBACK

A professional athlete always has a team around him/her: a coach, trainer, business manager, someone who takes care of the equipment, and a travel coordinator. S/he also has a massage therapist and a nutritionist. Everyone accepts that athletes need help and expertise to excel. Most entrepreneurs don't have a team to provide them with the resources they need to produce a stellar performance.

The late UCLA basketball coach John Wooden was brilliant when it came to understanding the power of teamwork. Author and leadership expert John C. Maxwell wrote about Wooden's skillfulness in a 2011 article in *Success* magazine: "Coach Wooden was a master at selecting players, and he knew how to motivate each person to fulfill his role on the team. Coach Wooden told me he recruited a lot of average shooters. But he also knew each player had a spot on the floor where they shot the best…Everyone had a role, and the majority of his players mastered their roles on the team. Wooden said, 'Teamwork is not a preference; it's a requirement.'"

Obtaining resources doesn't necessarily have to cost a lot of money. For example, my nutritional adviser is the guy who runs my vitamin store. He's had the same training as most nutritionists who charge an hourly fee. The key is to empower the team to provide you with feedback that's not only positive but also negative.

"Hey, Sebastiaan," my nutritional adviser told me the other day, "you're always complaining you're tired, but when was the last time you stepped on a scale?"

Right away, I stepped up my workouts and cut back on high-sugar fruits. The magic happens with granting empowerment. Feedback is always a killer resource. The key is to be able to accept feedback without judging the sender. If you judge the sender, s/he will stop giving feedback and never argue with you. Just say thanks when you receive feedback. Because, however painful, it is truly a gift, so treat the giver appropriately.

Yet just as you shouldn't summarily reject feedback, you shouldn't automatically accept it either. Get in the habit of taking your time when it comes to evaluating whether the feedback is appropriate for you and whether you should act on it.

A DOOMED ENVIRONMENT

A cell phone entrepreneur I mentored was struggling with fostering growth and revenue at his company.

We had lunch and then headed over to his office for a meeting. The building was located in an ugly industrial zone. We had to park on a broken-down curb. The owner had forgotten his key card, so he pressed the intercom outside the door, but nobody picked up. He finally called someone on his cell. When the employee came down, he snarled at us and said, "Man, I don't like opening front doors."

We headed up to the second and third floors (he'd been forced to close the first floor because of layoffs). We walked up a creaky spiral staircase, and as we circled up, I saw all these little separate rooms in which people were working. They peeked at us suspiciously as we ascended. The vibe felt closed and secretive and one of ducking and avoiding responsibility. The air reeked of disharmony. All the equipment was antiquated.

I advised the owner to update his equipment and move everyone to the ground floor, which was a big open space. I recommended he install flexible desks, which would force people to work together.

He told me he was worried employees would leave if he made them do that.

"Well, if people want to leave an open culture, let them leave," I said.

He said again that he was afraid if he lost people's knowledge and experience, he would cripple the company. Every decision he was making was out of fear and not out of strength.

"Well, if the company is going to be crippled by that, let it be crippled," I said.

He ignored both my suggestions, and the company ended up going bankrupt. It was a culture where change was virtually impossible, and the company just couldn't provide the most advanced products for the most competitive prices.

Takeaway: It's your job as an entrepreneur to provide people with the right resources, and if you don't, they will eventually fail.

I mentored one woman who started a platform for coaches. Early on, I realized she lacked the technical knowledge to grow the platform. She was relying on the knowledge of her tech provider. She also felt alone at the top. After three mentoring sessions, we agreed the best route for her would be to merge her platform with her tech provider. She was able to do so and gained a chief technology officer and a much-needed ally and sparring partner.

THE TRUTH ABOUT MONEY

Many times, people tell me their start-up idea isn't working because "there's not enough money out there to fund me."

"There's always money because money is scalable," I respond. "There's more money out there than start-ups need funding."

Remember the made-to-measure suit company I told you about in chapter four? I invested in an entrepreneur building a network of traveling tailors that was very much in demand at that time. We funded him with a huge marketing budget, fancy office space, and premium cars. He not only lacked the focus I previously discussed, but he also lacked team-building skills. He was incapable of hiring the go-getters whom the start-up desperately needed. The company failed within a year because his team wasn't focused on revenue growth.

When you believe money is an issue as a resource, it's a red flag that something else is the issue. Something is wrong with your business model. Or you're not good at pitching. It's never the fault of your customer or would-be investors. It's a symptom of another problem, and you need to diagnose what that is. If you can't do it, find someone as a resource who can.

CHAPTER SEVEN
FIFTH FACET: HEALTH

FOR MONTHS AFTER I GOT OUT OF THE HOSPITAL, I woke up exhausted every day. It wasn't your standard brand of exhaustion, like when you need a good night's sleep and to lay off the Red Bull and espresso shots. I was so tired all the time that I could barely tie my shoelaces.

I went to one medical doctor after another to try and find out why.

"Emotionally now, I'm doing great," I'd tell them, "but physically, I really think there's something wrong with me." After every medical work-up, doctors would say the same thing:

"Mr. Hooft, you're as healthy as a horse."

I didn't believe them. I really believed I had a disease or a serious medical condition. The doctors thought it was all in my head. But I knew it wasn't. I couldn't play soccer with my kids or even ride for a few minutes on my son's skateboard. By nine each night, I was ready for bed, but often I'd be too tired to sleep and lie awake wide-eyed all night.

Around Christmas, one of my friends posted a message on Facebook saying:

"I've just watched this documentary on a guy who drinks juice all day," and went on to rave about the health benefits the juicer had experienced.

The man in the documentary, titled *Fat, Sick, and Nearly Dead*, was Joe Cross, and he's changed my life as well as countless other people's.

Australian entrepreneur Joe Cross was one hundred pounds overweight and dealing with a severe autoimmune disease and the side effects of multiple steroids to treat it when he embarked on a personal quest to get his health back. Regular doctors had been unable to help him. So Joe decided to drink only fresh fruit and vegetable juice for sixty days as he drove three thousand miles across the United States. Joe regained his health, got off all his pills, and reversed his medical condition.

In January I went out, bought a slow juicer, and started juicing every day. The first nine days were hell. On day ten, I woke up, got out of bed, opened the curtains, and walked out onto my balcony. The Amstel River, which runs through Amsterdam, goes past my house. I looked at the river and squinted. It was a brighter blue than I had ever seen before. I looked at the trees. The leaves were in Technicolor. When I heard the birds singing, I heard each note of their musicality in a new way. Day ten showed me the connection between my mental health and my physical health.

I juiced for sixty days, just like Joe, and lost more than sixty pounds. I had more energy and was more clear-headed than I had ever been in my life. I found Joe on LinkedIn and sent him a note thanking him, and we ended up becoming digital friends. He inspires me with his contagious generosity. We've gone through similar transformations, from being single-focused, insanely unhealthy entrepreneurs to using our skills to build a better quality of life not only for ourselves but for as many people as possible in our spheres.

I learned how to listen to my body. The body is a well-organized instrument that will give you all the signals you need about how and what to eat. For example, the fresh produce you buy in the supermarket has been grown and treated in order to give it a long shelf life. A long shelf life means more profit for supermarkets and most growers. Even if you eat those fresh veggies and fruits all day, the nutritional intake won't be as great as locally grown and organic produce.

From Joe, I learned that there's no way to become a truly

successful entrepreneur on every level without your physical health. In the five years since Joe's documentary was released, twenty-five million people have watched it, and at least one million people have done Joe's "Reboot."

THE EFFICIENCY OF REBOOTING

by Joe Cross

First, let's define what a Reboot is. It's a period of time—fifteen days or more—where you consume only plant food, more specifically fruits and vegetables, when you extract the water that's trapped in those fruits and vegetables so it's just the juice coming out. So we're in some respects mimicking a water fast. (We're adding the plant's nutrients, micronutrients, sugars, and other phytonutrients to the water.) In that mimicking of a famine, the individual after three days generally finds a huge amount of clarity in the mind. There's a certain awareness; the senses are on high alert because they're trying to help you find food. That's the survival mechanism that comes up when you go on a famine. These survival mechanisms or modes include better eyesight, better hearing, better sense of smell, better taste, and better focus. That better focus really plays into someone who is an entrepreneur and can zero in on breaking through problems and clutter. A lot of us spend time down in the weeds. We're just hacking away trying to find our path in the forest. Every now and then we have to climb a tall tree to make sure we're in the right forest. Doing a Reboot is my definition of climbing a tall tree.

To be a very successful entrepreneur, you need to have three things going for you. It's really four, but three are in your control. The first thing is you need to be able to understand that you're going to have to take risks. And taking risks causes stress. Certain people have stresses that relate to food. When I get stressed, sugar comes into play for me. For some people, it's alcohol and drugs. Other people it's smoking. We're all different. But for a lot of people, stress equals poor habits and food.

The second thing you need to do is make huge sacrifices. You've got to give up a lot of effort and a lot of time when it comes to what you might like to be doing—fun things with friends and family, even exercise, because you are singularly focused on the work that has to be done. It's a 24-7 commitment.

The third thing is successful entrepreneurs have to be passionate about what they're doing. That passion can lead to health habits that aren't necessarily great because you're so passionate about what you're doing, you're caught up in it. It's that singular focus. And we all know what happens if you focus on just one thing: the things around it that need attention can come under threat.

The fourth thing entrepreneurs need for their success is luck. Luck plays a huge role. I'm not sure how much luck plays into your health and nutrition except where you're born, what country, and how your parents brought you up.

The single biggest goal that most entrepreneurs strive for

is efficiency. The Reboot is all about efficiency. Nutrition plays a huge role in the efficiency of our brains, thoughts, minds, and our resilience to stress. And of course, it helps our sleep. Sleep is critical for success in business. It's very difficult to operate on no sleep. We have to understand that many of our foods have chemicals in them that are inhibiting our thought processes. If I gave you a bottle of Jack Daniels, you wouldn't be thinking too straight after that bottle. It also stands to reason that many foods that we're eating also create irritation and frustration in the brain, and focus can dissipate. There are the mood swings, there are the afternoon lulls where your sugar levels have dropped because you've had two cans of soda or a plate of pasta at lunchtime, and now you're not going to be very productive as your body does battle with the insulin imbalance.

They've Got Our Bliss Points

The configuration of the world we've created around us—with technologies like elevators, escalators, automobiles—takes a lot of the energy we would normally expend out of play. On the food side, we have this new category called processed food. Seventy years ago, we never had that category. We had only plants and animals. Throughout our evolution, we have craved sugar, fat, and salt, and they have been quite difficult to come by, particularly the sugar and the fat. Now there's a term called the bliss point—it's when your brain responds to the perfect combination of sugar, fat, and salt. Many corporations today have configured their products to hit our bliss point, and they are super successful!

Many of us, not just through diet but also through over-prescription of antibiotics and other foods we're eating where the animals have been given antibiotics, are depleted from the healthy bacteria we need in our guts to assimilate food and keep us disease-free. Unless you're putting a lot of plant food in your system, it's very difficult for your gut to create any kind of balance. That's where we see an enormous amount of inflammation. Inflammation starts in the gut and spreads throughout the whole body. Inflammation is the root cause of so many diseases.

The Reboot's not a silver bullet. I call it time travel. You go back in time to our ancestors who used to go through periods of feast and famine, and the Reboot is the famine part. The feast part we've got well handled. If you think about it, there's a feast on every corner. Our job is to create this famine, which is a trip down memory lane for the body. I believe we should be doing five-day, ten-day famines two or three times a year to give our bodies a break and a chance to clear out and clean out what we're keeping too much of. When you have that break, when you release that pressure, the results are extraordinary. You're not putting in the stuff that was causing inflammation. You're allowing your body a chance to repair itself. I use the example: When you're out on your skateboard when you're a kid and you fall over and graze your knee, what does the body do? It heals itself; it forms a scab, that scab dries out, and over time the tissue regrows if it's left alone for a few weeks. It will repair, and it's back to good as gold. But if you pick at it two, three times a day, every day, it is not going to heal. It's going to get worse. It could get infected. You could get septicemia, lose your leg, and lose your life. As long as we get out of our own way and let the body heal itself, it can do it. If that can happen on the outside, why can't that happen on the inside? So many people have incredible benefits from a Reboot, whether that's healing migraines or skin, gut, and joint issues.

You're Your Own Expert

It's important to define what is healthy for you. For me, being healthy is two things: one is getting the data and the report card back from science: blood tests, measurements, heart rate, using all the technology we have to make sure we're in the guidelines defined by science. The next thing is we don't all need to have washboard stomachs and Victoria's Secret swimsuit bodies. Many people can be 20 percent overweight and be very happy and healthy. It's not just a case of if you're thin, you're healthy, and if you're fat, you're unhealthy. The second way I define being healthy is being able to do all the things I want to do with ease. Those things include riding a bike, going for a hike, swimming a mile, getting a good night's sleep, and being able to get up and down from the floor. The emphasis is on ease.

There are lots of tools and technology out there to measure health and fitness. Personally, I just use my own measurement: my level of happiness. That really dictates how much effort you need to expend. Once you get in tune, you know when you're off the rails, you know when you've indulged too much: a little too much sugar, a little too much fat, a little too much salt. You might recognize that after a day or a week, hopefully not after a month. We have these built-in mechanisms to protect us. It does require discipline, but it's really more about habit than about discipline. It's more about routine. It takes effort. You have to plan. You can't just wake up and go to a meeting and forget about breakfast and lunch and expect to find this incredible organic salad somewhere when they're serving only pizza. You've got to be organized.

The danger of using data to measure our health is that we can become disconnected from our own spirit, which is the best judge of where we are in our journey.

We all have playbooks for how we react to things. Breaking those playbooks is really difficult. This is the part—the changing of yourself, the letting go—that's frightening. Change equals discomfort for many people. But I think entrepreneurs look at change equaling opportunity. You've got to focus on the opportunity. I don't have a solution or an answer for how you let go of an old identity, but it's about how much you want to change. Old identities can also be changed by self-love. A lot of people don't love themselves. You need to start to appreciate yourself and love yourself. I'm not talking about posting a thousand selfies a day. I'm talking about giving yourself a break and not having that early-morning conversation about how ugly or fat or old or sick you are. The more you love yourself, the more you look after yourself.

Entrepreneurs are born leaders. As a leader, you have the eyes on you. You have people following you. So setting an example in this area is important. It's putting those philosophies into the workplace, such as ensuring that in your office you don't have the soda machine and the snack bar; you have the healthier options. Look for your office space to be located where there are healthier restaurants and parks. If your staff can get on the same wavelength as you, you're going to get more efficiency from them. That's only going to be better for the bottom line.

FINANCIAL HEALTH

I used to grocery shop on one of the poshest streets in Amsterdam. When I'd turn onto the block in my Porsche, retailers would look out the windows of their shops and say happily, "Great! There's Sebastiaan, and he's going to spend a couple of hundred euros in our store again."

After I embarked on my life redesign, I read the invoice for my laundry service for the first time. "Wow," I said to my girlfriend, "a thousand euros a year, that's really a lot for getting our clothes clean."

"That's our monthly invoice," my girlfriend replied.

When I got out of the hospital and started selling my businesses and redesigning my life, I couldn't afford to pay $4 for a single organic orange anymore. I had to do my own laundry.

First, it was hard, a big blow to my ego. People have a myth that every successful entrepreneur is financially astute when it comes to having money put away for a rainy day. They think all entrepreneurs have a cushion of savings and investments. It's simply not true. You can be great at generating value as an entrepreneur and horrible at generating an intelligent financial plan for the long term. I know it seems incongruent, but it's true, and the newspaper headlines about bankrupt celebrities and rap stars are proof.

The mentality I had in my old life was something like, "I'm making a lot of money right now. Why worry about the future?"

But to be a healthy entrepreneur, you have to think not only about making money for today but also about making money for tomorrow.

The money your business is generating is not your personal income. They are as different as the stars and the sky. Related but very different.

Whether you are intent on building a lucrative business or already own one, that doesn't mean you'll become rich or you are rich. You still must live within your means and steer clear of the unholy mayhem of consumption and consumerism. You must still design investments and create savings to cushion the fall when stuff happens, and stuff always happens. Maybe the risk-taking and creative nature of being an entrepreneur leads to impracticalities when it comes to designing a down-to-earth financial plan. I'm not sure. But what I do know for sure is that you can't eat rocks, as they say in real estate about being house rich and cash poor.

In addition, your net worth can never be the basis for your self-worth. Otherwise, you're setting yourself up for disaster if your business is sold or goes south. Your emotions will go haywire, and you'll lose your identity. If you see yourself and your business as one entity, then if it goes bankrupt, you will go bankrupt inside yourself.

MAKING CONGRUENT CHOICES

Remember my friend Sri (from chapter one) who owned a real estate company specializing in short-stay apartments in San Francisco? Sri wanted to be a market leader. He came to me for advice about how to run his business to achieve that aim. I told him what he needed to do was hire a team to help grow the business: Sri needed a call center, cleaning people, and a maintenance staff.

Before our discussion, Sri's focus was that he wanted more revenue, more apartments, "more of everything."

But as we talked further, we discovered his deepest desire was to have a high-quality, low-stress life with his family doing fun stuff. He wanted to take them on day trips up north on the weekends. When he became aware that living that kind of life wasn't congruent with big-city stress and the responsibilities of managing a large team, our discussion changed.

"Maybe it might be better to invest in bigger properties up north," he said, "so I can take my family there on the weekends and combine the lifestyle I want with managing my investments."

It was an important realization for Sri because it matched his underlying needs for emotional well-being. Sri had thought because he lived in San Francisco, he should build a business in San Francisco. But he ended up growing his business by buying and managing vacation properties in wine country. He figured out first what he needed to maintain and grow emotional health and built his business goals around that.

Two of Sri's best friends, Rafael and John, did the same thing. They went from being hard-core, hard-drinking real estate guys, right out of *Glengarry Glen Ross*, to owning a country inn an hour north of San Francisco called Park Winters in Winters, California. (They specialize in destination weddings.) They wanted their focus to be on quality of life. I've visited them a couple of times. The first day I met them, they took me to a local taqueria where they were regulars. The second day, I poached their land for fresh produce and found herbs, lemons, tomatoes, and figs. I made pasta and a salad with all the fresh ingredients. It was an eye-opener for them. Today, they sell their fresh produce locally (the fig jam is a favorite). Now, they're more in touch not only with their dream to create a country resort but also with their own health.

FIND OUT WHAT YOU REALLY WANT

Most entrepreneurs I meet don't realize that their well-being is dependent on the people around them. At work, your team will always try and please you, often in the guise of friendship, because you're the leader. It's critical to separate out friendship from your professional relationships. It's unfair to the people you're leading and inappropriate when it comes to fulfilling your own basic human needs. You'll never know if it's truly authentic.

The biggest mistake I see people making in their personal lives is they simply aren't clear with their loved ones about what they need and want. This may seem like a simplistic example, but all my family and friends know that I love the sun. No, let me rephrase that. I need the sun! It rains more than two hundred days of the year in Amsterdam. My friends and family invite me to go to the beach, the park, and to hang out outside. They do not invite me to go skiing. I have trained them not to. Sure, sometimes I feel left out when I see pictures of them cavorting in the snow on Snapchat, but I know what I need to be happy, and they do, too.

Whether it's personal or professional, so many of us have been trained to go along to get along. It starts early. For example, my daughter has to thank her teacher for the instruction each day at school before she can leave the classroom and go home. It's something I actually worry about because who knows if the teacher has done a good job that day? What if the programs that my daughter's studying don't fit her values or the way she learns best? Why should she thank someone for that, and what is that teaching her about how to communicate what she needs in personal and professional contexts?

Most of you reading this book attended a school designed to teach the average individual (whoever that is). But as a society, we're rapidly becoming more individual. There's a disconnect between the way we want to be and the way we're programmed. It's vital for you to understand that as you go about redesigning your life. You've got to stand firm when you start to feel guilty or uncomfortable about your specific life needs.

When I mentor people, I try to get them to find out what is really important to them. Quinn ran a start-up that is a division of a big corporation. I kept pressing Quinn to answer one question: "What will make you happy?" All he did was talk about how great his start-up was going to do and how much revenue it was going to generate. As we dug deeper, he started talking about how he really wanted to improve as an entrepreneur. Then Quinn discussed how much he wanted to be visible in the media discussing entrepreneurship. Finally, he realized that what he desired was to be a well-respected thought leader on growing start-ups. What Quinn needed in life didn't match what his corporation wanted, which was to make more and more money. So he began to go about trying to take the start-up out of the corporation and run it independently. Instead of being "the sales guy" all day, he also learned how to write and talk about entrepreneurship.

Every day, people go to work, and when they come home, they're asked, "How was your day?"

The response, in one way or another, is that their work makes them tired. Why would you want to do work that tires you?

Communicate, communicate, communicate. Tell yourself, your loved ones, and the people in your workplace what's important to you. If you don't, you'll drift like a cloud and become confused. One year becomes two and then three, four—eight years can go by with you ending up completely burned out.

METRICS AND FEEDBACK

Living a healthy life is a decision. It doesn't come easy, and you need ways to remind yourself how to stay on course. Hundreds of online tools exist to track everything from productivity to physical, mental, and emotional health. It's important to find your own way of tracking your progress in multiple arenas. I've created several dashboards on my desktop that provide me with metrics in categories such as financial health and my social media impact. The key to health is also planning daily, weekly, and monthly feedback sessions with yourself and your mentor network on what you're trying to achieve.

One of the ways to reach and maintain great health is to give your team of mentors permission to provide feedback, the importance of which I also stressed in chapter six about the Resources facet. Managing my weight, for example, is a constant issue for me. I hate going to the gym, but I do it. Not too long ago, I lapsed and didn't go to the gym for a month. When I returned, the first thing my personal trainer said to me was, "Did you go swimming this morning?"

"No," I replied.

"Then what is that inner tube doing around your middle?" he said.

Ouch. But he motivated the hell out of me, and we worked out a plan to get my weight back on track.

It's all about creating a process for measuring physical, emotional, and financial health.

YOU MAY NEED TO TAKE IT SLOW

When you're an entrepreneur, many of your friends are managers, CEOs, and other entrepreneurs. These people are ambitious, and they are always busy. Idleness is not cool.

When I redesigned my life, I decided that in order to maintain optimal health, I needed to work six to eight hours a day max. The first day I tried the new work schedule, I decided to go swimming in the morning. I went to an indoor, public pool near my house, bought a ticket for €5, and changed into my gear.

I swam one lap and then the second. As I started the third lap, I glanced up at the clock; it said five minutes to nine. Nine is the standard time to start work in the Netherlands. I stopped swimming. I felt paralyzed because I felt so guilty about not going to work. I actually sank to the bottom of the pool.

I went home and threw away my swim gear (which, for your information, was too small anyway). I told myself, *It's too soon, too fast*, when it came to making such a radical change. My body was physically attached to starting work at that time. Eventually, I was able to reach the six-to-eight-hour workday, but it took a while. Whatever new component you're trying to implement to ignite your health, you might need to ease into it.

One of the benefits of working a shorter day is that I've stopped doing things that are irrelevant. If you are working a twelve-to-fourteen-hour day, there's a good chance you're solving problems that aren't your job to solve. If you let them, problems often solve themselves.

When I mentor people who work overly long days, I ask them to write down everything they get accomplished in a workday for two days straight. They will inevitably come back to me with a piece of paper with about three things on it.

"It feels like I'm doing more," they'll protest.

If this is you, that's a sign you're heading on the road to burnout. You feel like you're really busy, but in fact, you're becoming more inefficient. Prioritizing details is a dangerous state to be in because you lose sight of the big picture. It's time to sit down and balance your time over the Five Facets and get back to seeing the forest, not only the trees.

I KNOW YOUR WORLD

Most of the books I've read on entrepreneurship, whether they are how-to books or biographies, are written from what I call a peacetime perspective. The author retired or sold his/her business and then moved to someplace like Miami or La Jolla to write his/her book on entrepreneurship from his/her deck chair by the pool or the ocean. The problem is the life these people are currently living has nothing to do with the life you're currently living.

I am betting you, like me, are in what I call, again, the rush hour of life. You have a spouse or significant other, kids, and a sweet but needy dog or cat (or both), and most of the time, your house feels crazy because everything is happening at once. You Skype into client meetings wearing a button-down shirt (for professional appearances) and your pajama bottoms. You have dried cereal in your shoes. You go to bed and get up in the same day (like 1:00 a.m. and 5:00 a.m.).

I had to figure out how to be an entrepreneur in a way that it wasn't the only thing that mattered. I wrote this book so you could, too. The Five Facets, working together, address all the issues you're facing in real time. The facets aren't just a model to follow but also a way to live your life. They're interconnected, like the organs in the human body, and when they function in concert, you have optimal health. When you focus on what you like to do and what you're good at, momentum builds and your intention becomes a self-fulfilling prophecy.

In the Netherlands a few years ago, we had a conference called FailCon, where everyone talked about what they learned from their failures. That's not normally my style of motivating people because in the end, nobody wants to fail. What I've learned is that failure is more about asking questions than about not succeeding. When you find out *why* you failed, you are less likely to do so in the future. Asking questions in the service of creating a different outcome reframes the entire experience.

Living the Five Facets gives you a model from which to ask yourself questions about how to live the life you, and only you, are meant to live. Every single decision I make today, small and large, stems from that single moment in the hospital where I decided to live a happy, meaningful, and purposeful life. It was a choice, and the simplicity of that still astonishes me. As I said in the beginning, I flipped the switch, and you can, too. Not today, not tomorrow, but right now.

CONCLUSION

I LOOKED OUT FROM THE STAGE and blinked into the blinding lights. Five hundred people were on their feet applauding. We were in the sleek, modern auditorium at Iceland's Arion bank. I had just finished a talk on sustainable entrepreneurship. I couldn't believe how far I'd come in a few years.

After the lights came up, a line of people approached the stage, and I answered more questions. It took more than an hour. Finally, one gentleman remained.

At first look, I could tell he was a businessman and an extremely successful one. He was in his midforties, sporting a smart haircut with perfectly graying temples; he could have been an Italian model showing off a custom-made suit. (It was one of the most expensive suits I'd ever seen.) He looked like the kind of guy who drove an Audi A8 home to a perfect blonde wife and matching children who attended the best schools in Reykjavik. Most of all, the guy looked like he was in control.

He approached me and then turned around to see if anyone else remained in our vicinity. We were alone. He looked up at me and said quietly, "Thank you for opening my eyes."

He was silent for a few moments. Then he started crying. The tears did not stop. It was just tears and tears and tears punctuated by sniffling.

"Finally, someone has confronted me with the fact that everyone around me is happy, my family, my employees, but I feel empty," he said. "I'm exhausted. Finally, someone showed me—you showed me—that I need to take care of me instead of always taking care of other people. I never understood this, but now I understand. Thank you."

Then he quickly turned around and walked away.

It's a cliché that it's lonely at the top, but clichés exist for a reason. As I interviewed five hundred entrepreneurs across the globe for this book, after about a half hour of conversation, most of them told me how lonely they feel. When I responded by telling them that was a cross-global experience, most were surprised. They thought they were the only ones. Nobody wants to tell anyone because s/he is scared of appearing weak. It's a code of silence, one that has serious ramifications for entrepreneurs' health, well-being, and success.

When it comes to redesigning our own lives, we all possess codes of silence, with ourselves and the people close to us. But only by breaking them can we turn the page. Then the past will be prologue, as Shakespeare said.

FROM "ME" TO "WE"

Today, as I mentioned in chapter three, I'm an international DJ. I connected with my first love, music, and redesigned my life.

Recently, I was talking with the manager of a big dance act. He said, "It's amazing how someone who is forty years old, with everything against him PR-wise, was able to build such an impressive catalog of tracks and gigs in just under eighteen months."

"Thank you," I replied, grateful for the acknowledgment.

"I've never, ever seen anyone do that," he said. "How did you do it?"

I told him about the Five Facets and how I built a team to support me.

"Yeah, you're always talking about *we*," he said. "*We* are doing this, and *we* are doing that. Most of the artists I deal with are always talking about *me* instead of *we*. Some artists have to work years and years to learn what you just told me in five minutes."

As you know, I used to be one of those people who always thought they could do everything alone. Even when I was with other people—having lunches, meetings, drinks—there was still a sense that I was alone. I needed a mentor.

A mentor would have pointed out to me that despite my staggering financial success and celebrity visibility, I wasn't doing that well personally. A mentor would have given it to me straight. Your partner and your family are there to love you, not necessarily to give you advice.

Please go about finding a team of mentors; it will transform your life. One of the ways to find excellent mentors is to inspire experts with your questions. For people at the top of the Entrepreneur's Pyramid, it's always refreshing to meet someone who surprises you with what they want to know and who possesses that curious, lively, infectious energy that you had when you were starting out. It's easy to want to mentor people like that. I'd also like to extend an invitation for you to connect with me. (I'm on all the social networks; it's not hard to find me.) I would be happy to receive your questions, and I promise to provide answers to help you become a happy, healthy, and successful entrepreneur.

Finally, I'd like for you to think of this book as one of your mentors, a guide for your new world. I wish you (and your team) the best on your journey.

ACKNOWLEDGMENTS

THIS BOOK IS FOR MY FATHER, Gé Hooft, with love and gratitude. I'd also like to dedicate it to my kids, Enzo and Senna; I want you to know that you can redesign your life at any time. Thank you to Leslie Guttman, for the terrific editing and for all the ideas, input, and support; and to my publisher Jeremy Brown, who showed me that I can always write a second book. Heartfelt thanks to Nyenrode Business University program manager Ger Zwartendijk, who played an instrumental role in the development of the canvas. Other thanks go to Frank Buytendijk at Gartner for motivating me to write this book. Special thanks to my best friend, Michaël Ferron, for seeing me for who I am. Also, much gratitude to Michaël, a celebrated international artist, for the cover art (titled *Promise,* created in 2000), which represents a promise that you, too, can redesign your life. Thank you to Joe Cross for bringing back health into my life and for writing a special section for you, the reader.

ABOUT THE AUTHOR

SEBASTIAAN HOOFT founded twenty companies in fifteen years as one of the Netherland's top tech entrepreneurs and was listed among the country's one hundred most successful self-made entrepreneurs by the Dutch business magazine *Quote*. Hooft speaks globally on entrepreneurship and is a respected thought leader in the field, featured by TEDx and such publications as *U.S. News & World Report*. His twin passion is music, and Hooft is currently an international DJ while also working as a mentor to dozens of start-ups, guiding them through the principles outlined in *Redesign*.

www.ingramcontent.com/pod-product-compliance
Lightning Source LLC
Chambersburg PA
CBHW031947190326
41519CB00007B/702